The
Scuppernong Press

Wake Forest, NC

Living in the Land of Cotton Biography Series

Thomas Jonathan "Stonewall" Jackson

By
Richard Lee Montgomery

Living in the Land of Cotton Biography Series
Thomas Jonathan "Stonewall" Jackson

©2017 Richard Lee Montgomery

First Printing

The Scuppernong Press
PO Box 1724
Wake Forest, NC 27588
www.scuppernongpress.com

Cover and book design by Frank B. Powell, III

All rights reserved. Printed in the United States of America.

No part of this book may be reproduced or transmitted in any form or by any means, electronic or mechanical, including photocopying, recording, or by any information and storage and retrieval system, without written permission from the editor and/or publisher.

International Standard Book Number ISBN 978-1-942806-12-7

Library of Congress Control Number: 2017946964

Living in the Land of Cotton Biography Series

— Table of Contents —

Introduction to Series..*iii*

Thomas Jonathan "Stonewall" Jackson...................................... 1

Jackson's Formative Years.. 5

Jackson's Military Years 9

The Cause For Which Jackson Fought..................................... 21

Bibliography 27

ii — Thomas Jonathan "Stonewall" Jackson

— Introduction to Series —

As a member of the Sons of Confederate Veterans and for every other member, we have been charged to stand in *"the defense of the Confederate soldier's good name, the guardianship of his history, the emulation of his virtues, the perpetuation of those principles which he loved."* Through my website, the books I have published and the lectures I have given, are all about keeping the Confederate culture alive in this cynical time of America's history.[1]

For my life, I have committed it to living a lifestyle which would be pleasing to the Lord Jesus Christ. However, knowing that I can easily displease Him and therefore diminish His glory, there are foundational tools which have been a constant reminder for me in seeking to glorify my God. Seeking to live for the Lord Jesus Christ, I have learned to strive in developing a prayer life and equally allowing a healthy time in the reading of the Word of God, which can bring direction and focus.

My point is, this can easily describe many of the leaders of the Confederacy as well as those on the battlefield as soldiers. In fact, the Confederate Constitution teaches to us what was of most importance to them, *"We, the people of the Confederate States, each State acting in its sovereign and independent character, in order to form a permanent federal government, establish justice, insure domestic tranquility and secure the blessings of liberty to ourselves and our posterity — invoking the favor and guidance of Almighty God — do ordain and establish this Constitution for the Confederate States of America."*[2]

---

[1] livinginthelandofcotton.com
[2] Constitution of the Confederate States of America (Milledgeville: Georgia State Convention, 1861), 2.

Thomas Jonathan "Stonewall" Jackson

I find the phrase *"invoking the favor and guidance of Almighty God,"* as a foundational statement in this new constitution. It teaches us there was a culture which was very important to the South before, during and after the years of 1861-1865. In this new series of biographies, the reader will see that there were men and women who fought for the protection of their families, homes, towns, cities, states and country by an invading army. The reader will see there were those who held to Christian principles and at the same time, fought for States' Rights and held this principle high.

I am not suggesting that this new government was a Christian (theocratic) nation because there were many who were not Christians, but who also fought for States' Rights. Also, there were many who did not know anything about this constitutional right issue — they just knew they did not want anyone dictating to them and their families what they can and cannot do.

This series is based on primary sources. By that I mean they are books published before "Lincoln's War" and books published going into the 1930s. Much of what you will read are quotes and narratives from these sources. At times, I will interject my thoughts but centered on what the source stated. The desired outcome for this new series is that the reader might be inspired, encouraged and become more proactive for the truths of history.

I hope you enjoy this biography,

Richard Lee Montgomery

Living in the Land of Cotton Biography Series

Thomas Jonathan "Stonewall" Jackson

Born: January 21, 1824 in Clarksburg, Virginia.

Wives: Eleanore Junkin and Mary Anna Morrison.

Children: Julia Laura Jackson.

Death: 3:15 PM, May 10, 1863, Guinea, Virginia.

Buried: Stonewall Jackson Memorial Cemetery, Lexington, Virginia.

"He often declared that it was his first desire to command a 'converted army.' This, he believed, enjoying the spiritual favour of God upon their individual souls, engaged in a just cause, and undertaking every enterprise with prayer, must meet with success, and prove in the end invincible." [3]

---

[3] Robert L. Dabney, *Life of Lieut.-Gen. Thomas J. Jackson* (London: James Nisbet & Company, 1866), 423.

Living in the Land of Cotton Biography Series

Pershing

"On June 18, 1920, **General John J. Pershing**, while at Lexington, VA, placed a wreath upon the grave of General Robert E. Lee, and delivered a brief address, during which he said that Lee was one of the world's greatest generals. Veterans of the Civil and World War stood at attention during the ceremonies. General Pershing then visited the tomb of General Thomas Jonathan Jackson, and declared that 'the world looked on him and his accomplishments with admiration and awe.'"[4]

George G. Higgins of Captain Snowden Andrews Battery, says of Jackson: "His men loved him. They would go anywhere he ordered them, for they believed, as I have often heard them say, that when he took them in he could take them out. They not only were willing to do what he said, but loved to carry out his orders. No man ever had the love of his soldiers like Stonewall Jackson.'"[5]

Edward Alfred Pollard of the *Richmond Examiner* wrote, "When Jackson was prostrated with his wound that unexpectedly proved mortal, Gen. Lee sent him a number of kindly messages in his peculiarly simple and affectionate words. 'Give him,' he said in his half-playful and tender

Pollard

manner, 'my affectionate regards, and tell him to make haste and get well, and come back to me as soon as he can. He has lost his left arm, but I have lost my right arm.' At another time, hearing of the threatening change in the condition of the sufferer, he said with great feeling: 'Surely Gen. Jackson must recover. God will not take him from us, now that we need him so much. Surely he will be spared to us, in answer to the many prayers which are offered for him.' He afterwards added: 'When you return, I

---

[4]Elihu S. Riley, *Stonewall Jackson: A Thesaurus of Ancedotes of and Incidents in the Life* (Annapolis, Md.:, 1920), 188.
[5]Ibid., 26.

Living in the Land of Cotton Biography Series

trust you will find him better. When a suitable occasion offers, give him my love, and tell him that I wrestled in prayer for him last night, as I never prayed, I believe, for myself.'" [6]

A. J. Emerson of Denver, who wrote *articles for the Confederate Veteran* magazine in the early 1900s stated in the Volume 20 Issue, "*Was Stonewall Jackson a faultless man? No; but he was one of the world's greatest generals, and his fame reflects honor upon all the people of the Southern States, if not of the whole United Slates.*" [7]

Stonewall Jackson was well loved and respected by many around the world. Why — because he was a principled man. Jackson had a high regard for duty. You would hear him say, "*Through life let your principal object be the discharge of duty.*" [8] "*Disregard public opinion when it interferes with your duty.*" [9] He also had a high regard for respect, "*Never speak disrespectfully of anyone without a cause.*" [10] "*Make no expense but to do good to others or yourself; waste nothing.*" [11] But like anyone else, Jackson had his enemies but history teaches us that Jackson was respected and admired by most. We would do well to emanate the life of Thomas Jonathan Jackson.

Jackson

---

[6]Edward Alfred Pollard, *Lee and His Lieutenants: Comprising the Early Life, Public Services, and Campaigns of General Robert E. Lee and His Companions in Arms, with a Record of Their Campaigns and Heroic Deeds* (E. B. Treat & Company, 1868), 122-123.
[7]S. A. Cunningham, *Confederate Veteran*, Volume 20 (Nashville, 1912), 58.
[8]Mary Anna Jackson, *Life and Letters of General Thomas J. Jackson* (New York: Harper & Brothers, 1892), 35.
[9]Elihu S. Riley, *Stonewall Jackson: A Thesaurus of Ancedotes of and Incidents in the Life* (Annapolis, Md.;, 1920), 35.
[10]Ibid., 35.
[11]Ibid., 36.

Living in the Land of Cotton Biography Series

Living in the Land of Cotton Biography Series

— Jackson's Formative Years —

*J*ackson was born in the town of **Clarksburg, Virginia**, on January 21, 1824. He came from Scotch-Irish stock. Thomas' father and mother, **Jonathan** and *Julia Neale Jackson* lived in Upshur County. *"Thomas had one brother, Warren, and two sisters, Elizabeth and Laura. Not long after the birth of Laura, Elizabeth was taken ill with fever and died. The father, worn out with nursing, also took the fever; two weeks after the child's death he was laid in a grave by her side. On settling Jonathan Jackson's affairs, it was found that he had left no property for his widow and babes."* [12]

Birthplace of Stonewall Jackson

Jonathan

Thomas was six years old when his mother *Julia* remarried, to a Blake Baker Woodson on November 4, 1830. The *Jackson family* did not approve of this marriage for his reputation was *"fond of company and good living, but always hard run for means"* and also had eight children and was twenty-eight years Julia's senior. The family threatened to take the children in order to ensure their well-being, as well as their educa-

---

[12]Mary L. Williamson, *Life of Thomas J. Jackson* (Atlanta: B. F. Johnson Publishing Company, 1918), 11-12.

tion. In short order, *Julia and her husband Blake were "unable to support her children in comfort."* [13]

In this next narrative we see the tragedy of a family having to separate because of financial difficulties. *"The eldest son, Warren, was a rebellious boy, and his short life was full of unhappiness. The daughter, more fortunate in her home than either of her brothers, grew to womanhood in the house of an aunt. Little Thomas went from his mother to live with a sister of his father, and his adopted home was near Clarksburg. He remained there a year, a quiet and subdued child. For some reason his uncle was stern to him, and one day, when only eight years old, he, without saying a word to any one, walked the four miles that lay between his home and Clarksburg, and unannounced appeared at the house of Judge Jackson, a cousin of his father's, and asked Mrs. Jackson for his dinner.*

Warren & Thomas

The child as he sat at the table, calmly eating the food that was placed before him, said to his hostess, 'I have quit Uncle Brake; we don't agree, and I shall not go back any more.' His cousin expostulated with him, and tried to persuade him to return. He declined to do so, and this cousin permitted him to leave her house for that of another relative in the town. At this relative's house he stayed all night, and there made the same announcement that he should return no more to his uncle's home. The strange indifference of these relatives to the little wanderer cannot be explained. The child was a mere babe in years, and yet they let him go from them, the last one knowing that he proposed to walk a journey of eighteen miles to where his brother was, and yet opposed no objection and apparently offered no assistance.

---

[13]R. P. Chew, *Stonewall Jackson Address of Colonel R. P. Chew, Chief of Horse Artillery, Army of Northern Virginia* (Lexington, VA: *Rockbridge County News Print*, 1912), 4.

Living in the Land of Cotton Biography Series

The long journey was accomplished at last, and Thomas reached the home of his uncle, Cummins (Edward) Jackson, where he had the pleasure of being united to his brother again. The uncle was a father to the two boys, and four years were passed happily in his house. Then the unhappy disposition of the eldest brother caused trouble, and on his refusal to attend school regularly his uncle became indignant. The lad announced his determination to leave his adopted home, and his relative not only permitted him to go, but to take his brother, then twelve years of age, with him." [14]

Side note: *While the boys lived with their uncle for a year, in 1831, Julia die of ill health. It was said that, "Much of the talent her children possessed they inherited unmistakably from her. She was extremely religious, and was naturally a happy person."* [15]

Now, returning to the narrative: *"The two children, not knowing what else to do, went to the house of an uncle of their mother's. They were hospitably treated, but the disobedience of the eldest brother again caused a quarrel, and he left this home taking with him the now thoroughly wretched Thomas."* [16]

"Long months passed before the children were heard of again. They went down the Ohio River on a flatboat, and then down the Mississippi until they reached a lonely island opposite the south-western corner of Kentucky. They had earned their food by first one occupation and then another until they landed on this island, and there they cut wood for the Mississippi. ... A kind-hearted steamboat captain who knew them gave them their passage back to Virginia, and little Thomas, thoroughly sick of his experiences and determined not to be subjected to his brother's will any longer, returned to his uncle's home and was welcomed back by his relatives. Warren sought a home with his aunt, Mrs. Brake, with whom

---

[14] Laura C. Holloway, *The Mothers of Great Men and Women, and Some Wives of Great Men* (Baltimore: R. H. Woodward & Company, 1892), 249-250.
[15] Ibid., 245.
[16] Ibid., 250.

Thomas had made his first home, and died of consumption, which disease had been developed by his hardships. Thomas never left his Uncle Cummins again until he went to **West Point**." [17]

West Point

---

[17] Ibid., 250-251.

Living in the Land of Cotton Biography Series

— Jackson's Military Years —

In the year of 1842 young *Jackson* was eighteen years old. A vacancy at the United States Military Academy, at West Point opened up. After meeting with Mr. **Samuel Lewis Hays**, member of Congress from his district, he took young Jackson to meet with the Secretary of War **John Canfield Spencer** and was met with approval and ordered that his entrance papers to West Point be made out at once. There were fifty-nine freshmen or plebes, who entered the Academy in 1842. Names you might be familiar with are Dabney Herndon Maury, George B. McClellan, Samuel Bell Maxey and George E. Pickett.

Hays

Spencer

Mary Lynn Williamson, in her 1918 published work entitled, *Life of Thomas J. Jackson* writes, **"While at West Point, Jackson wrote a number of rules for his own guidance.** They touched on morals, manners, dress, the choice of friends, and the aims of life. One of them should be known to every boy It reads, 'You may be whatever you resolve to be.' We shall see that this was indeed the guiding star of Jackson's life. He did what he aimed to do by force of will, and by that will power he raised himself from a poor country boy to be one of the most famous men of his age.

Living in the Land of Cotton Biography Series

Jackson entering West Point

At this time of his life, it is plain that it was Jackson's purpose to place his name high on the roll of earthly honor. Beneath his shy and modest manner, there burned within him the desire to be great. His life was not yet ruled by religion, but it showed many high and noble aims.

*He was twenty-two years old when he left West Point, on June 30, 1846. He at once took the rank of second lieutenant of artillery in the United States service. The artillery is that branch of the army which fights with cannon, or big guns. At this time a war was being waged between Mexico and the United States. General **Winfield Scott** was about to go to the seat of war as the commander-in-chief of the United States army. Jackson, the young lieutenant, was sent to join him in the south of Mexico."* [18]

Scott

Here are some accounts of *Thomas J. Jackson's* bravery in Mexico. *"In the battle of Churubusco Jackson first won distinction. Magruder's battery was assigned to a post within nine hundred yards of the enemy's works. His first lieutenant, Mr. Johnstone, falling early in the action, Jackson took his place and became second."* [19] This is what *Magruder* reported of *Jackson,* *"In a few moments Lieutenant Jackson, commanding the second section of the battery, which had opened fire upon the enemy's works from a position on the right, hearing our fire still farther in front, advanced in handsome style, and, being assigned by me to the post so gallantly filled by Lieutenant Johnstone, kept up the fire with great briskness and effect. His conduct was equally conspicuous during the whole day; and I cannot too highly commend him to the*

---

[18] Mary L. Williamson, *Life of Thomas J. Jackson* (Atlanta: B. F. Johnson Publishing Company, 1918), 26-28.
[19] Sarah Nicholas Randolph, *The Life of Gen. Thomas J. Jackson* (Philadelphia: J. P. Lippincott & Company, 1876), 37.

major-general's favorable consideration. For his gallantry in the battle of Churubusco, Jackson received the brevet rank of captain."[20]

"He soon had another chance to show his skill and courage. The army crossed the mountains to the strong castle of Chapultepec, which was built on a high hill overlooking the plain leading to the City of Mexico. The level fields at the foot of the mountain were covered with crops of grain and groves of trees. Here and there were deep ditches that the farmers had dug for drains. These ditches, which the artillery and horsemen could not cross, were so hidden by the growing crops and bushes that they could not be seen by the soldiers until the guns had reached them.

The castle of Chapultepec was held by large numbers of Mexican troops, while cannon were placed to sweep every road leading up to it. On September 13, the American troops made an assault on Chapultepec from three sides at once.

Jackson, with his guns, took part in the attack on the northwest side. Two regiments of footmen, or infantry, went with him. The light artillery pressed forward, pouring shot and shell into the foe, until it came close to the Mexican guns. At this short range Jackson soon had many of his men and horses struck down by the storm of grape-shot.

Jackson Lifting A Gun

General Worth, seeing that Jackson was hard pressed, sent him word to fall back. But the young officer replied that he would take the guns which were doing such deadly work if General Worth would only give him fifty more men. While he was waiting for this force, **Jackson lifted a gun across a deep ditch** with the help of one man and opened fire on the Mexicans. The other soldiers of his command were killed, wounded, or seeking shelter in the ditch.

---

[20] Ibid., 37-38.

Living in the Land of Cotton Biography Series

Another cannon was moved across the ditch, and in a few minutes the Mexicans gave way before the fire of the two guns. By this time, the troops attacking the castle on the other sides had succeeded in fighting their way in, and the Mexicans began to fall back on the City of Mexico." [21]

For his bravery Jackson was promoted to the rank of major. At the end of the Mexican War, Major Thomas J. Jackson was sent with his command to Fort Hamilton, Long Island and was stationed there for two years. From there he was sent to Fort Meade, Florida. *"Jackson had not been many months at Fort Meade when he was relieved from the irksome life there by being elected* **Professor of Natural Philosophy and Artillery Tactics in the Virginia Military Institute at Lexington.***"* [22] I want you to hear what *Mary Lynn Williamson* gives in her narrative: *"General* **Francis H. Smith,** *long superintendent of the Virginia Military Institute, wrote thus of Jackson's election as professor: 'It is not surprising that when the Board of Visitors of the Institute were looking about for a suitable person to fill the chair of natural philosophy and artillery tactics, the friends of the brave young major should have pointed him out as one worthy of the honor. Other names were laid before the Board of Visitors by the faculty of West Point, all of them of men noted for scholarship and gallant services in Mexico. McClellan, Reno, Rosecrans, afterwards generals in the Northern army, and G. W. Smith, who became a Confederate general, were thus named. But the fitness of young* **Jackson,** *the high testimonials to his character, and the fact that he was a native Virginian satisfied the Board that they might safely choose him for the chair without seeking candidates from other States.*

Jackson the Professor

Smith

---

[21] Mary L. Williamson, *Life of Thomas J. Jackson* (Atlanta: B. F. Johnson Publishing Company, 1918), 31-32.
[22] Sarah Nicholas Randolph, *The Life of Gen. Thomas J. Jackson* (Philadelphia: J. P. Lippincott & Company, 1876), 43.

Living in the Land of Cotton Biography Series

He was therefore elected on March 28, 1851, and took up his duties in September." [23]

While establishing himself in Lexington — *"Two important events mark this period of Jackson's life — his marriage and profession of religion. He married **Miss Junkin**, daughter of the Rev. Dr. Junkin, President of Washington College, This lady did not long survive her marriage, and her only child, a daughter, died in infancy. Several years after the death of his first wife he was again married to **Miss Morrison** of North Carolina. By this marriage he had one child, Julia, born a few months before his death. Jackson became a member of the Presbyterian church of the town, then under the charge of an excellent old man, the Rev. Dr. White. ... he speedily became an active and prominent member of the church, and filled, during his residence at Lexington, important secular positions in it. Every Sunday, with military regularity, the figure of the Professor was seen in his pew at the Presbyterian church, hymn-book in hand, his earnest countenance turned up to the pulpit with close attention. Religious duties soon became the controlling occupation of his life; the society of good men and women his chief relaxation and greatest source of pleasure."* [24]

Mary Anna Morrison

Eleanor Junkin

Jackson was tall, slender and reticence to express his views. Also, he was stiff and unbending with most people and possessed of an intense Presbyterian religious faith. However, conflict seemed to be no bother to him, for on one occasion as professor, *"a cadet, sent away from the Institute because of something that had happened in Jackson's classroom,*

---

[23]Mary L. Williamson, *Life of Thomas J. Jackson* (Atlanta: B. F. Johnson Publishing Company, 1918), 38-39.
[24]John Esten Cooke, *Stonewall Jackson* (New York: G. W. Dillingham, Publisher,1893), 21-22.

Living in the Land of Cotton Biography Series

became so angry that he challenged the major to fight a duel. He sent word that if Jackson would not fight he would kill him on sight. Jackson refused to fight the duel; but he let the youth know, through his friends, that if he were attacked he would defend himself. The attack was not made, in spite of the fact that Jackson passed back and forth through the streets as usual.

James Alexander Walker

The cadet who had challenged him was under Jackson's command in the War Between the States, and rose to be the leader of the famous Stonewall Brigade. In later years when asked his opinion of the great general, he said that Jackson was the only man who had never been beaten." [25] This cadets name was **James Alexander Walker**, who became Brigadier General and was granted a honorary degree in 1872, in recognition of his Confederate service.

On December 20, 1860, South Carolina took the lead to withdrawn their allegiance from the United States. The domino effect began with one Southern state after an other, withdrawing or succeeding from the Union. *"On the 9th of February, 1861, a Provisional Government was formed at Montgomery, Alabama, for a Confederacy composed then of the States of South Carolina, Mississippi, Alabama, Georgia, Louisiana, and Texas. Jefferson Davis was chosen President, and Alexander H. Stephens Vice-President, of this Confederacy."* [26]

Finally on February 19, Virginia seceded from the Union as well. With Lincoln's proclamation on declaring war against South Carolina and the Confederate Government and calling upon the States for seventy-five thousand men to form an army of invasion. Now, *"Virginia bent all her energies to make preparations for defense against the armies which were being rapidly enrolled to invade the South. As the news of her secession spread from one part of the country to the other, her sons belonging*

---

[25]Mary L. Williamson, *Life of Thomas J. Jackson* (Atlanta: B. F. Johnson Publishing Company, 1918), 45-46.
[26]Ibid., 55.

Living in the Land of Cotton Biography Series

to either the army or the navy of the United States speedily resigned their commissions and hurried home to offer their services to their mother State, believing their first duty belonged to her. ... Foremost among her distinguished sons was Colonel **Robert E. Lee**. When the news reached Richmond that he had resigned his commission and had declared his resolution never again to draw his sword save in defense of his native State, men who were oppressed by the impending dangers breathed more freely." [27]

Colonel Lee

At this point, *"Colonel Lee was appointed by his State major-general and made commander-in-chief of her forces. In organizing the material for her defense, one of his first steps was to form camps of instruction, the chief of which was on the outskirts of Richmond, and called after him Camp Lee. It was decided to call to this camp from the Virginia Military Institute the elder cadets, who could act as drillmasters and assist in organizing into an army the patriotic but untrained troops who poured in to offer their services in the defense of the country. On **Major Jackson** devolved the duty of taking the cadets to Richmond."* [28] *"The cadets marched to Staunton, and went thence by rail to Richmond. From a depot east of the Blue Ridge, where their journey was interrupted for a short time. Major Jackson wrote to his wife, 'Here, as well as at other points of the line, the war-spirit is intense. The cars had scarcely stopped here before a request was made that I would leave a cadet to drill a company.' Having reached Richmond, he wrote to Mrs. Jackson, April 23, 'Colonel Lee, of the army, is here, and has been made major-general. His services I regard as of more value to us than General Scott could render as commander.'"* [29]

Major Jackson

---

[27] Ibid., 57-58.
[28] Ibid., 58.
[29] Ibid., 60.

Living in the Land of Cotton Biography Series

Colonel Jackson

On April 27 **Jackson was commissioned as Colonel** and was ordered to take command at **Harper's Ferry**, which he did on May 3, 1861. *"Jackson was assigned to the command of a brigade of infantry, composed of four regiments of Virginians."* [30] Suffice it to say, Jackson was a born leader. From Second Lieutenant to Colonel. Then on July 3, 1861 *Jackson receives a letter, "My dear General, 'I have the pleasure of sending you a commission of Brigadier-General in the Provisional Army, and to feel that you merit it. May your advancement increase your usefulness to the State.' Very truly, **R. E. Lee**."* [31]

Harper's Ferry

Robert E. Lee

Another promotion came, for *"On the 7th of October, 1861, the Minister of War rewarded General Jackson's services at Manassas with promotion to the rank of Major-General in the Provisional Army. The spirit in which this new honor was received, is displayed in the following letter to his wife: — 'October 14th, 1861.— It gives my heart an additional gratification to read a letter that hasn't travelled on our holy Sabbath. I am very thankful to that good God who withholds no good thing from me (though I am so utterly unworthy and so ungrateful), for making me a major-general of the provisional army of the Confederate States. The commission dates from October 7th. 'What I need is a more grateful heart to the 'Giver of every good and perfect gift.' I have great reason to be thankful to our God for all His mercies which He has be-*

---

[30] John Esten Cooke, *Stonewall Jackson: A Military Biography* (New York: D. Appleton & Company, 1876), 37.
[31] Mary L. Williamson, *Life of Thomas J. Jackson* (Atlanta: B. F. Johnson Publishing Company, 1918), 77.

16 — Thomas Jonathan "Stonewall" Jackson

Living in the Land of Cotton Biography Series

stowed, and continues to shower upon me. Our hearts should overflow with gratitude to that God who has blest us so abundantly and over-abundantly. O that my life could be more devoted to magnifying His holy name!"

There was, however, another day that brought a greater joy to his life, the birth of his daughter. *"On the 23rd of November, 1862, God blest him with a daughter. To a man of his extreme domesticity and love for children this was a crowning happiness; and yet, with his great modesty and shrinking from publicity, he requested that he should not receive the announcement by telegraph, and when it came to him by letter he kept the glad tidings all to himself leaving his staff and those around him in camp to hear of it through others."* This new born baby's name was **Julia**.[32]

Julia Laura Jackson

Soon after this joyous occasion came the Battle of Fredericksburg, in December of 1862. From December 1862 to March 1863 Jackson made his winter-quarters at Moss Neck. And then in May of 1863 came with the **Battle of Chancellorsville**. Date: May 2 — Time: 9:00 p.m. — *"Night had fallen. About eight o'clock General Jackson rode forward with two or three of his staff along the plankroad, and advanced one hundred and fifty yards in front of his foremost skirmishers, peering with those keen eyes which you might fancy could be seen through the densest gloom forward into the night. He turned to ride back — a **heavy fire from one of his own regiments**, hailing from North Carolina, but whose number I will in mercy withhold, saluted him. One bullet struck his left arm*

Jackson Attack on Federals at Battle of Chancellorsville

---

[32]Mary Anna Jackson, *Memoirs of Stonewall Jackson By His Widow, Mary Anna Jackson* (Louisville: The Prentice Press, 1895), 360.

Living in the Land of Cotton Biography Series

Wounding of Jackson

four inches below the shoulder, shattering the bone down to the elbow. The wound was intensely painful; he half fell, half was lifted from his horse. An aid galloped back to A. P. Hill to report that **Stonewall Jackson was wounded and lying in the road. General Hill galloped hastily up, flung himself from the saddle,** *began, choked with emotion, to cut the cloth of Jackson's sleeve, when suddenly four of the Federal videttes appeared on horseback, and were fired on by the staff-officers. The videttes fell back upon a strong and swiftly advancing line of Federal skirmishers. General Hill and all the officers and couriers of both staffs had no alternative but to mount and ride for their lives, leaving Jackson where he lay. Right over the ground where was stretched the wounded lion the Federals advanced. Within their grasp lay the mightiest prize, the most precious jewel in the Confederate crown; but it was not destined that Stonewall Jackson should be struck by a Federal bullet, or yield himself prisoner to a Federal soldier. As General Hill and his companions galloped back they also became the*

General A. P. Hill binds the wounds of Stonewall Jackson

target of the same luckless North-Carolinians. General Hill's boot was cut by a bullet, but his leg uninjured; Colonel Crutchfield, Chief of Artillery to Jackson, was seriously if not mortally wounded; Boswell, of Jackson's staff, killed; Howard, Engineer to A. P. Hill, knocked from his horse, but whether killed, or wounded, or a prisoner, is not known; two or three couriers killed. Without losing a moment, General Hill threw his own skirmishers forward, backed by heavy supports, **and the ground on which lay General Jackson was again occupied by the Confederates.** *But in the*

Death Wound of Stonewall Jackson

Living in the Land of Cotton Biography Series

mean time two more bullets, both from his own men, had struck him as he lay on the ground, one passing through the wrist of his shattered arm, the other entering the palm of his right hand and coming out through its back. He was at once carried to the rear and his arm instantly amputated under chloroform." [33]

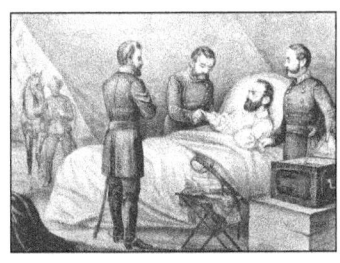

The Death of "Stonewall" Jackson

General Jackson was moved to a field hospital at the home of Thomas and Mary Chandler, approximately 30 miles from the *battlefield*. **It would be on May 10 that *Jackson* died at 3:15 p.m.** We are told that, *"On his death-bed, when his hours were numbered, and his spirit drifted slowly toward eternity, the pale lips opened, and he murmured in a whisper: 'Bury me in Lexington, in the Valley of Virginia!'"* [34] In his last words *"after, a sweet smile overspread his face, and he murmured quietly, with an air of relief: 'Let us cross over the river and rest under the shade of the trees.' ... without any expression of pain, or sign of struggle, his spirit passed away."* [35] On May 15 **Jackson's funeral** took place in Lexington, Virginia.

Jackson's Funeral, VMI

---

[33] Markinfield Addey, *The Life And Military Career Of Thomas Jonathan Jackson, Lieutenant-General In The Confederate Army* (New York: Charles T. Evans, 1863), 207-208.
[34] John Esten Cooke, *Stonewall Jackson* (New York: G. W. Dillingham, Publisher,1893), 21.
[35] H. M. Wharton, *War Songs And Poems Of The Southern Confederacy, 1861-1865* (1904), 180.

Living in the Land of Cotton Biography Series

— The Cause For Which Jackson Fought —

It is a known fact that Jackson was not a secessionist but he had a great love and affection for his home State of Virginia. Jackson's wife **Mary Anna** perhaps says it best, *"At this time Major Jackson was strongly for the Union, but at the same time he was a firm States' rights man. In politics he had always been a Democrat, but he was never a very strong partisan, and took no part in the political contest of 1860, except to cast his vote for* **John C. Breckinridge**, *believing that his election would do more to save the Union than that of any other candidate. He never was a secessionist, and maintained that it was better for the South to fight for her rights in the Union than out of it."* 36

Mary Anna Morrison Jackson

John C. Breckinridge

It is true that Jackson favored the union and questioned the wisdom of secession but he also believed that individual states had rights that should be respected and that secession was legitimate if it were used for protecting them. *Mary L. Williamson gives this narrative: "Major Jackson was truly Southern in feeling. He believed in the 'Rights*

36Mary Anna Jackson, *Life and Letters of General Thomas J. Jackson* (New York: Harper & Brothers, 1892), 139.

Thomas Jonathan "Stonewall" Jackson — 21

of States' and also that the South ought to take her stand and resent all efforts to coerce and crush her. He, however, dreaded war and thought it the duty of Christians throughout the land to pray for peace.

William S. White

A month before South Carolina went out of the Union, Major Jackson called upon his pastor, **Dr. White,** *and said: 'It is painful to know how carelessly they speak of war. If the Government insists upon the measures now threatened, there must be war. They seem not to know what its horrors are. Let us have meetings to pray for peace.' Dr. White agreed to his request, and the burden of Major Jackson's prayer was that God would preserve the land from war."* [37]

But the greatest affection that steered Jackson's life — his desires — his thinking and his convictions was the love for his Lord Jesus Christ, who had imputed His righteousness in his soul. In his book entitled **The Religious Life of Famous Americans,** Louis Albert Banks gives us this narrative on Jackson's conversion to Christianity: *"The commanding officer of his regiment while it was in Mexico following the Mexican War, Colonel Francis Taylor, was the first man to speak to Stonewall Jackson on the subject of personal religion. Taylor was an earnest Christian, constantly interested in the religious welfare of his soldiers. He made a deep impression on young Jackson, who after this conversation resolved to study the Bible and seek all the light within his reach.*

On his return to the United States, soon after settling as a professor at the Virginia Military Institute, Lexington, VA, he applied for admission

---

[37] Mary L. Williamson, *The Life of Gen. Thos. J. Jackson In Easy Words For Youth* (Richmond: B. F. Johnson Publishing Company, 1899), 83.

into the Presbyterian Church, making a public profession of his faith in Christ on November 22, 1851. He soon became a deacon in the church, and with a soldier's training in obedience to superior command he followed out the same principles in his church duties, going to his pastor as his chief for his 'orders,' and 'reporting' performance of them in a military way.

Few men had such reverence for ministers of the Gospel as had Jackson, and he often said that, had his education fitted him for it and had he more of the gift of speaking, he would have entered the pulpit." [38]

Throughout more than one hundred and fifty years, there have been illustrations given to demonstrate the prayer life of Thomas Jonathan Jackson. The first illustration is taken from Mary Lynn Williamson's published work entitled **The Life of Gen. Thos. J. Jackson In Easy Words For Youth**: *"His corps moved forward, and, on August 9th, fought the battle of Cedar Run. In this fierce battle one of the regiments began to fall back. At that instant Jackson placed himself at the head of the column, drew his sword, and cried in a voice of thunder, 'Rally, brave men! Jackson will lead you! Follow me!' This turned the tide of battle, and the Federal army broke into full retreat. Just before this battle, some officers enquired of 'Jim,' the General's servant, if there were any signs of a battle. 'Oh, yes, sir,' replied he, 'the General is a great man for praying night and morning, all times; but when I see him get up in the night and go off and pray, then I know there is going to be something to pay; and I go right straight and pack his haversack, for I know he will call for it in the morning.'"* [39]

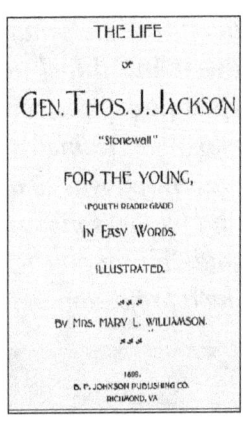

---

[38] Louis Albert Banks, *The Religious Life of Famous Americans* (Boston: American Tract Society, 1904), 125-126.
[39] Mary L. Williamson, *The Life of Gen. Thos. J. Jackson In Easy Words For Youth* (Richmond: B. F. Johnson Publishing Company, 1899), 183-184.

Living in the Land of Cotton Biography Series

Richard S. Ewell

The second illustration is seen with Jackson praying and **General Richard Stoddert Ewell** looking on. Taken from the 1888 published work entitled *Christ in the Camp: Or, Religion in Lee's Army* by **Dr. John William Jones**, we are told, *"I have it from a well-authenticated source that the conversion of Lieutenant-General Ewell, Jackson's able lieutenant, was on this wise: At a council of war, one night, Jackson had listened very attentively to the views of his subordinates, and asked until the next morning to present his own. As they came away, A. P. Hill laughingly said to Ewell, 'Well! I suppose Jackson wants time to pray over it.' Having occasion to return to his quarters again a short time after,* **Ewell found Jackson on his knees and heard his ejaculatory prayers for God's guidance** *in the perplexing movements then before him. The sturdy veteran Ewell was so deeply impressed by this incident and by Jackson's general religious character, that he said: 'If that is religion, I must have it;' and in making a profession of faith not long afterwards he attributed his conviction to the influence of Jackson's piety."* [40]

J. William Jones

White

A third illustration of Jackson's complete dependence on the God of the Bible, is told to us by **Henry Alexander White**, *"When Jackson opened his eyes, after a long, quiet slumber, on Sunday morning, May 3rd, the battle around Chancellorsville was at its height. ... Jackson called his chaplain, Beverley T. Lacy, to come and sit near him. 'You see me,' said the general, 'severely wounded, but not de-*

---

[40] John William Jones, *Christ in the Camp: Or, Religion in Lee's Army, Supplemented By A Sketch Of The Work In The Other Confederate Armies* (Richmond: B. F. Johnson & Company, 1888), 97.

pressed; not unhappy. I believe that it has been done according to God's holy will, and I acquiesce entirely in it. You may think it strange, but you never saw me more perfectly contented than I am to-day; for I am sure that my Heavenly Father designs this affliction for my good. I am perfectly satisfied, that either in this life, or in that which is to come, I shall discover that what is now regarded as a calamity is a blessing. I can wait until God, in His own time, shall make known to me the object He has in thus afflicting me. If it were in my power to replace my arm, I would not dare to do it; unless I could know it was the will of my Heavenly Father.

Preparing For Battle

'It has been a precious experience to me,' he said further, 'that I was brought face to face with death and found that all was well. I then learned that one who has been the subject of converting grace and is the child of God can, in the midst of the severest sufferings, fix the thoughts upon God and heavenly things, and derive great comfort and peace.'" [41]

This was the man — **Thomas "Stonewall" Jackson**. A Godly *man* — a *role model then* — and a *role model today*. We would be wise to keep in mind Jackson's favorite maxim was ... **"Duty is ours; consequences are God's."** [42]

---

[41] Henry Alexander White, *Stonewall Jackson* (Philadelphia: George W. Jacobs & Company, 1909), 355-356.
[42] Robert L. Dabney, *Life of Lieut.-Gen. Thomas J. Jackson* (London: James Nisbet & Company, 1866), 422.

Living in the Land of Cotton Biography Series

Living in the Land of Cotton Biography Series

— Bibliography —

Constitution of the Confederate States of America (Milledgeville: Georgia State Convention, 1861)

Addey, Markinfield, *The Life And Military Career Of Thomas Jonathan Jackson, Lieutenant-General In The Confederate Army* (New York: Charles T. Evans, 1863).

Banks, Louis Albert, *The Religious Life of Famous Americans* (Boston: American Tract Society, 1904).

Chew, R. P., *Stonewall Jackson Address of Colonel R. P. Chew, Chief of Horse Artillery, Army of Northern Virginia* (Lexington, Va.: Rockbridge County News Print, 1912).

Cooke, John Esten, *Stonewall Jackson* (New York: G. W. Dillingham, Publisher, 1893).

Cunningham, S. A., *Confederate Veteran*, Volume 20 (Nashville, 1912).

Dabney, Robert L., *Life of Lieut.-Gen. Thomas J. Jackson* (London: James Nisbet & Company, 1866).

Holloway, Laura C., *The Mothers Of Great Men And Women, And Some Wives Of Great Men* (Baltimore: R. H. Woodward & Company, 1892).

Jackson, Mary Anna, *Life and Letters Of General Thomas J. Jackson* (New York: Harper & Brothers, 1892).

Jackson, Mary Anna, *Memoirs of Stonewall Jackson By His Widow, Mary Anna Jackson* (Louisville: The Prentice Press, 1895).

Jones, John William. *Christ in the Camp: Or, Religion in Lee's Army, Supplemented By A Sketch Of The Work In The Other Confederate Armies* (Richmond: B. F. Johnson & Company, 1888).

Pollard, Edward Alfred, *Lee and His Lieutenants: Comprising the Early Life, Public Services, and Campaigns of General Robert E. Lee and His Companions in Arms, with a Record of Their Campaigns and Heroic Deeds* (E. B. Treat & Company, 1868).

Randolph, Sarah Nicholas, T*he Life of Gen. Thomas J. Jackson* (Philadelphia: J. P. Lippincott & Company, 1876).

Riley, Elihu S., *Stonewall Jackson: A Thesaurus of Ancedotes of and Incidents in the Life* (Annapolis, Md.:, 1920), 188.

Wharton, H. M., *War Songs And Poems Of The Southern Confederacy, 1861-1865* (1904).

White, Henry Alexander, *Stonewall Jackson* (Philadelphia: George W. Jacobs & Company, 1909).

Williamson, Mary L., *Life of Thomas J. Jackson* (Atlanta: B. F. Johnson Publishing Company, 1918).

Living in the Land of Cotton Biography Series

www.ingramcontent.com/pod-product-compliance
Lightning Source LLC
Chambersburg PA
CBHW050508120526
44588CB00044B/1851